A New Tune A Day ™

Performance Pieces
for Cello

Compiled and arranged by Ned Bennett
Cello advisor Janet Coles

Chord symbols for all pieces are included for
guitar or keyboard accompanime

Boston Music Company
part of The Music Sales Group
London/New York/Paris/Sydney/Copenhagen/Berlin/Madrid/Tokyo

Contents

Published by
Boston Music Company
Exclusive Distributors:
Music Sales Corporation
257 Park Avenue South, New York, NY 10010, USA
Music Sales Limited
8/9 Frith Street, London W1D 3JB, UK
Music Sales Pty Limited
120 Rothschild Avenue, Rosebery, NSW 2018,
Australia

This book © Copyright 2006 Boston Music
Company, a division of Music Sales Corporation.

Compiled and edited by Ned Bennett
Series Editor: David Harrison
Music processed by Paul Ewers Music Design
Cover and book designed by Chloë Alexander
Photography by Matthew Ward
Printed in the US
Backing tracks by Guy Dagul
CD recorded, mixed and mastered by
Jonas Persson and John Rose

Your Guarantee of Quality
As publishers, we strive to produce every book to
the highest commercial standards. The music has
been freshly engraved and the book has been
carefully designed to minimize awkward page
turns and to make playing from it a real pleasure.
Throughout, the printing and binding have been
planned to ensure a sturdy, attractive publication
which should give years of enjoyment. If your
copy fails to meet our high standards, please
inform us and we will gladly replace it.

www.musicsales.com

Camptown Races

Moderately

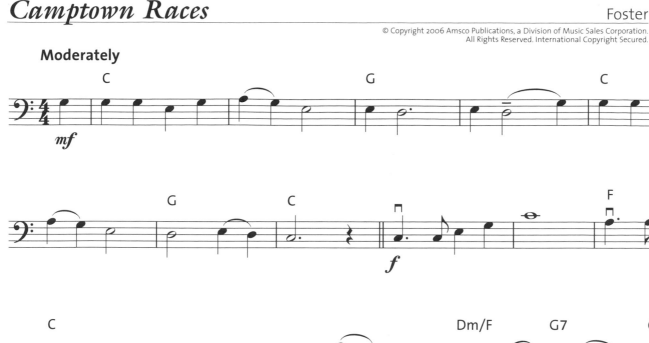

Early One Morning

Moderately

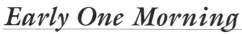

4 Santa Lucia

Neapolitan Traditional

Moderately

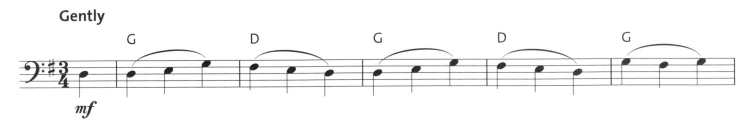

5 *Poor Little Buttercup* (from *HMS Pinafore*)

Sullivan

Gently

My Bonnie Lies Over The Ocean

Scottish Traditional

Smoothly

Romance No. 1

Beethoven

Smoothly

Kalinka

Moderato

Coventry Carol

Gently

Molly Malone

Yorkston

Banana Boat Song

Jamaican Traditional

12 *Telstar*

Meek

Moderately quick

Satin Doll

Ellington, Strayhorn & Mercer

Moderate swing

14 *Coasts Of High Barbary*

American Traditional

Fairly quick

15 *Babu Sau*

Ngizim Traditional

Lively

Mama Don't Allow

American Traditional

16

Lively swing

La Cucaracha

Mexican Traditional

17

18 *Shenandoah*

American Traditional

© Copyright 2006 Amsco Publications, a Division of Music Sales Corporation.
All Rights Reserved. International Copyright Secured.

19 *Turkey In The Straw*

American Traditional

© Copyright 2006 Amsco Publications, a Division of Music Sales Corporation.
All Rights Reserved. International Copyright Secured.

Steal Away

20

Slowly

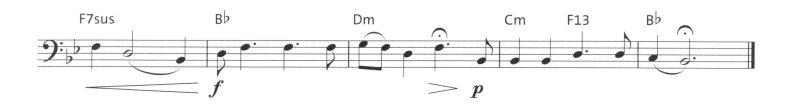

Over The Hills

21

Moderately

Catch A Falling Star

Vance & Pockriss

Moderate (Rumba)

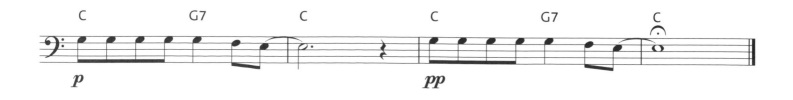

Underneath The Arches

McCarthy, Flannigan & Connely

Slow swing

24 ***Ding Dong Merrily On High***

16th Century French

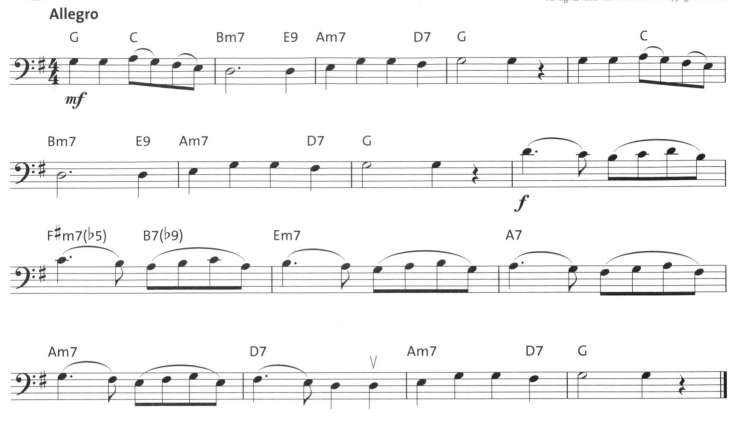

25 ***By The Rivers Of Babylon***

Caribbean Traditional

Old Folks At Home

Foster

Andante

Minuet

Bach

Poco allegro

28 *Jurassic Park Theme*

Williams

Angel Eyes

Brent & Dennis

Copyright © 1946 (Renewed) by Onyx Music Corporation (BMI).
All Rights Administered by Music Sales Corporation (ASCAP).
International Copyright Secured. All Rights Reserved.

Slow swing

30 *Dick's Maggot*

Scottish Traditional

Moderately

31 *Nobody Knows*

Burleigh

Slowly

British Grenadiers

British Traditional

32

Boldly

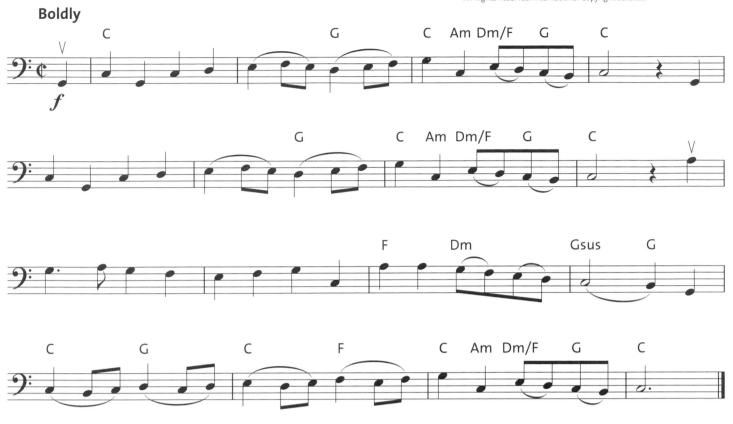

Minuet

Mozart

33

Allegretto

21

34 *Greensleeves*

English Traditional

Flowing

35 *The Hebrides Overture* (excerpt)

Mendelssohn

Andante espressivo

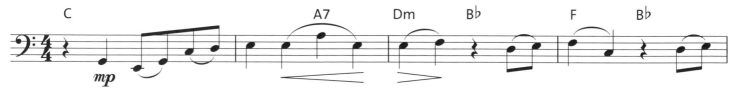

The Keel Row

36

Brisk (optional swing)

Mexican Hat Dance

37

To Coda

D.S. al Coda   Coda

38   *Perdido*

Tizol

Blackadder Theme

Goodall

Moderately

Deep River

Spiritual

Das Wandern

Zöllner

Hatikvah

Steadily

The Ash Grove

Moderately

44 Bill Bailey

American Traditional

Fast swing

45 Tit Willow (from *The Mikado*)

Sullivan

Moderato

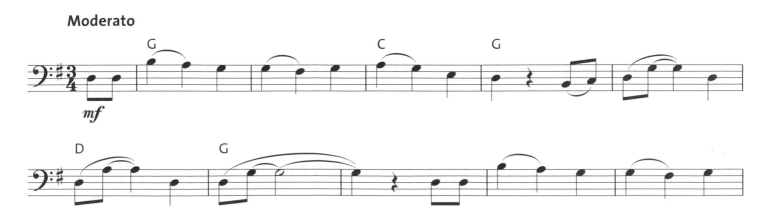

Waltz

Brahms

Moderately

47 *Men Of Harlech*

Moderato

48 *Rock-A-My Soul*

Spiritual

Moderate swing

Estampie

Lively

G and D throughout

We'll Meet Again

Parker & Charles

Moderate swing

Diamonds Are A Girl's Best Friend

Styne & Robin

51

Lively

52 *Jeanie With The Light Brown Hair*

Foster

Gently

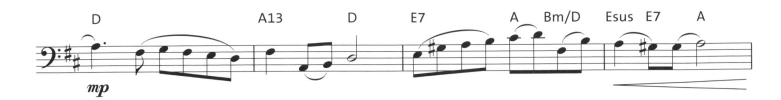

53 *Emperor Quartet* (excerpt)

Beethoven

Adagio

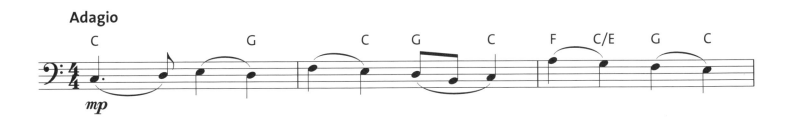

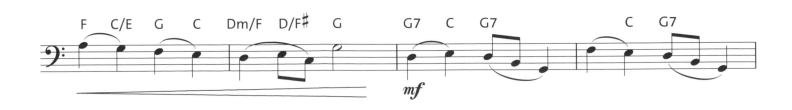

Swan Lake (excerpt)

Tchaikovsky

Andante cantabile

55 *Polovtsian Dance*

Borodin

Andante moderato

Dark Eyes

57 *Jupiter* (from *The Planets Suite*)

Andante

Bring Me Sunshine

Kent & Dee

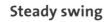

58

Steady swing

The Frim Fram Sauce

Ricardel & Evans

Moderate swing

Try A Little Tenderness

Woods, Campbell & Connelly

Moderate swing

Grand March (from *Aida*)

Verdi

Boldly

Radetsky March

Strauss

Moderato

63 *Nellie The Elephant*

Hart & Butler

Moderately

John Brown's Body

American Traditional

© Copyright 2006 Amsco Publications, a Division of Music Sales Corporation.
All Rights Reserved. International Copyright Secured.

Medium swing

In The Hall Of The Mountain King (from *Peer Gynt*)   Grieg   65

Fig Leaf Rag   Joplin   66

CD backing tracks

1	Tuning Note	**23**	Underneath The Arches	**45**	Tit Willow
2	Camptown Races	**24**	Ding Dong Merrily On High	**46**	Brahms Waltz
3	Early One Morning	**25**	By The Rivers Of Babylon	**47**	Men Of Harlech
4	Santa Lucia	**26**	Old Folks At Home	**48**	Rock-A-My Soul
5	Poor Little Buttercup	**27**	Bach Minuet	**49**	Estampie
6	My Bonnie Lies Over The Ocean	**28**	Jurassic Park Theme	**50**	We'll Meet Again
7	Romance No. 1	**29**	Angel Eyes	**51**	Diamonds Are A Girl's Best Friend
8	Kalinka	**30**	Dick's Maggot	**52**	Jeanie With The Light Brown Hair
9	Coventry Carol	**31**	Nobody Knows	**53**	Emperor Quartet
10	Molly Malone	**32**	British Grenadiers	**54**	Swan Lake
11	Banana Boat Song	**33**	Mozart Minuet	**55**	Polovtsian Dance
12	Telstar	**34**	Greensleeves	**56**	Dark Eyes
13	Satin Doll	**35**	The Hebrides Overture	**57**	Jupiter
14	Coasts Of High Barbary	**36**	The Keel Row	**58**	Bring Me Sunshine
15	Babu Sau	**37**	Mexican Hat Dance	**59**	The Frim Fram Sauce
16	Mama Don't Allow	**38**	Perdido	**60**	Try A Little Tenderness
17	La Cucaracha	**39**	Blackadder Theme	**61**	Grand March
18	Shenandoah	**40**	Deep River	**62**	Radetsky March
19	Turkey In The Straw	**41**	Das Wandern	**63**	Nellie The Elephant
20	Steal Away	**42**	Hatikvah	**64**	John Brown's Body
21	Over The Hills	**43**	The Ash Grove	**65**	In The Hall Of The Mountain King
22	Catch A Falling Star	**44**	Bill Bailey	**66**	Fig Leaf Rag

How to use the CD

The tuning note on track 1 is A.

After track 1, the backing tracks are listed in the order in which they appear in the book. Look for the ⊙ symbol in the book for the relevant backing track.

Listen for the clicks at the start of each track: depending on the tempo and time signature, each track will have clicks for one or two bars before the melody begins. When the melody starts with an anacrusis, the click will also play for the first part of the bar.